THE
BRITISH TRANSPORT
COMMISSION GROUP

FORMER THOMAS TILLING COMPANIES IN THE 1960s

THE
BRITISH TRANSPORT COMMISSION GROUP

FORMER THOMAS TILLING COMPANIES IN THE 1960s

JIM BLAKE

PEN & SWORD
TRANSPORT

Published in 2018 by
Pen & Sword Transport
an imprint of
Pen & Sword Books Ltd
47 Church Street
Barnsley
South Yorkshire
S70 2AS

ISBN 978 1 47385 722 3

Typeset by Matthew Wharmby

Printed and bound by Replika Press Pvt. Ltd.

Pen & Sword Books Ltd incorporates the imprints of Pen & Sword Archaeology, Atlas, Aviation, Battleground, Discovery, Family History, History, Maritime, Military, Naval, Politics, Railways, Select, Transport, True Crime, and Fiction, Frontline Books, Leo Cooper, Praetorian Press, Seaforth Publishing and Wharncliffe.

For a complete list of Pen & Sword titles please contact
PEN & SWORD BOOKS LIMITED
47 Church Street, Barnsley, South Yorkshire, S70 2AS, England
E-mail: enquiries@pen-and-sword.co.uk
Website: www.pen-and-sword.co.uk

COVER: **Several Tilling** Group companies with seafront operation had Bristol Lodekkas which could be converted to open-top during the summer. One such was Brighton, Hove & District. Here, their No.22, a 60-seat FS6B new in 1960 has come to London for a tour of the sights after the Epsom Derby where it had been in use as a grandstand.

BACK COVER: **It was** quite common for elderly buses to be cut down for use as open-toppers on seaside services. One of the most famous examples of this was Southern Vectis 1939 ECW-bodied Bristol K5G 56-seater No. 702 seen here at Shanklin. This one was particularly unusual in retaining its original pre-war bodywork, and has actually survived in use until the present century. It is preserved today.

CONTENTS

ABOUT THE AUTHOR

I was born at the end of 1947, just five days before the 'Big Four' railway companies, and many bus companies – including London Transport – were nationalised by Clement Attlee's Labour government.

Like most young lads born in the early post-war years, I soon developed a passionate interest in railways, the myriad steam engines still running on Britain's railways in those days in particular. However, because my home in Canonbury Avenue, Islington was just a few minutes' walk from North London's last two tram routes, the 33 in Essex Road and the 35 in Holloway Road and Upper Street, my parents often took me on these for outings to the South Bank, particularly to the Festival of Britain which was held there in the last summer they ran, in 1951. Moreover, my father worked at the GPO's West Central District Office in Holborn and often travelled to and from work on the 35 tram. As a result, I knew many of the tram crews, who would let me stand by the driver at the front of the trams as they travelled through the Kingsway Tram Subway. This was an unforgettable experience for a four-year-old! In addition, my home was in the heart of North London's trolleybus system, with route 611 actually passing my home, and one of the busiest and most complicated trolleybus junctions in the world – Holloway, Nag's Head – a short ride away along Holloway Road. Here, the trolleybuses overhead almost blotted out the sky! Thus from a very early age, I developed an interest in buses and trolleybuses which was equal to my interest in railways, and I have retained both until the present day.

I was educated at my local Highbury County Grammar School, and later at Kingsway College, by coincidence a stone's throw from the old tram subway. I was first bought a camera for my 14th birthday at the end of 1961, which was immediately put to good use photographing the last London trolleybuses in North West London on their very snowy last day a week later. Three years later, I started work as an administrator for the old London County Council at County Hall, by coincidence adjacent to the former Festival of Britain site. I travelled to and from work on bus routes 171 or 172, which had replaced the 33 and 35 trams mentioned above.

By now, my interest in buses and trolleybuses had expanded to include those of other operators, and I travelled throughout England and Wales between 1961 and 1968 in pursuit of them, being able to afford to travel further afield after starting work. I also bought a colour cine-camera in 1965, with which I was able to capture what is now very rare footage of long-lost buses, trolleybuses and steam locomotives. Where the latter are concerned, I was one of the initial purchasers of the unique British Railways 'Pacific' locomotive 71000 Duke of Gloucester, which was the last ever passenger express engine built for use in Britain. Other preservationists laughed at our group which had purchased what in effect was a cannibalised hulk from Barry scrapyard at the end of 1973, but they laughed on the other side of their faces when, after extensive and innovative rebuilding, it steamed again in 1986. It has since become one of the best-known and loved preserved British locomotives, often returning to the main lines.

Although I spent thirty-five years in local government administration, with the LCC's successor, the Greater London Council, then Haringey Council and finally literally back on my old doorstep, with Islington Council, I also took a break from office drudgery in 1974/5 and actually worked on the buses as a conductor at London Transport's Clapton Garage, on local routes 22, 38 and 253. Working on the latter, a former tram and trolleybus route, in particular was an unforgettable experience. I was recommended for promotion as an inspector, but rightly thought that taking such a job with the surname Blake was unwise in view of the then-current character of the same name and occupation in the On The Buses TV series and films, and so declined the offer and returned to County Hall!

By this time, I had begun to have my transport photographs published in various books and magazines featuring buses. I had also started off the North London Transport Society, which catered for enthusiasts interested in the subject. In conjunction with this group, I have also compiled and published a number of books since 1977, featuring many of the 100,000 or so transport photographs I have taken over the years.

Also through the North London Transport Society, I became involved in setting up and organising various events for transport enthusiasts in 1980, notably the North Weald Bus Rally which the group took over in 1984; it has raised thousands of pounds for charity ever since. These events are still going strong today.

In addition to my interest in public transport, I also have an interest in the popular music of the late 1950s and early 1960s, in particular that of the eccentric independent record producer, songwriter and manager Joe Meek. In Joe's tiny studio above a shop in Holloway Road (not far from the famous trolleybus junction) he wrote and produced Telstar by The Tornados, which became the first British pop record to make No.1 in America, at the end of 1962, long before The Beatles had even been heard of over there! When Joe died in February 1967, I set up an Appreciation Society for his music, which is still going strong today. His music has a very distinctive sound.

I also enjoy a pint or two (and usually more) of real ale. I have two grown-up daughters, Margaret and Felicity, and three grandchildren, Gracie, Freddie and Oscar, at the time of writing. I still live in North London, having moved to my present home in Palmers Green in 1982.

INTRODUCTION

During the 1960s, the Tilling Group of bus companies operated approximately half of the inter-urban and rural bus services in England and Wales, and had been nationalised by Clement Attlee's Labour Government in 1948 under the control of the British Transport Commission. Ownership passed to the Transport Holding Company Ltd in 1963, though the fleets remained under Tilling Group control.

In the period covered by this book, the operators within the group had very standardised fleets, with the vast majority of their buses and coaches having Bristol chassis and Eastern Coachworks (ECW) bodywork. This was a result of these manufacturers also having been nationalised and controlled by the BTC and THC. However, some Tilling Group operators still had earlier vehicles with, for instance, AEC or Leyland chassis which had been acquired prior to the requirement for them to buy only Bristol products, while some also had coaches with Bedford or Ford Thames chassis built in the 1950s and 1960s.

Unlike the BET fleets throughout England and Wales, most Tilling fleets also had highly standardised liveries, either of red with cream relief, or green with cream relief for their stage carriage buses, or the reverse of this for their coaches. There were some exceptions, though. The most obvious ones were Midland General and Notts & Derby, whose livery was an attractive dark blue and cream; as well as the Royal Blue coaches of Southern and Western National, and the maroon and cream coaches of Thames Valley subsidiary South Midland.

Sadly, to many bus enthusiasts, myself included, Tilling fleets in the 1960s were boring owing to the standardisation of liveries and vehicle types; though fortunately there were still many elderly vehicles in most of the fleets which in themselves were interesting.

In November 1967, the BET group of bus companies was bought out by the Tilling Group and all became part of the National Bus Company in early 1969, and before long these operators' distinctive liveries became just a memory when the NBC imposed standard red or green liveries on them much in the same way the Tilling Group had on their fleets.

Throughout most of the 1960s, I travelled to many of these operators and photographed their vehicles, often on Omnibus Touring Circle outings, as well as spending many summer Saturdays at London's Victoria Coach Station where their service buses as well as express coaches could be seen.

I was fortunate to have been able to have captured much of this changing transport scene on film, and am pleased to be able to present some more of my photographs in this volume. Most have never been published before. Unless otherwise stated in the text, all buses and coaches have Bristol chassis and Eastern Coachworks bodywork.

I must put on record my thanks to the PSV Circle, from whose records most of the vehicle details included herein are taken, as well as to my old friends Paul Everett and Ken Wright, who were often with me when I took the photographs all those years ago, and have helped refresh my memory regarding some of them. Also may I thank Colin Clarke and John Scott-Morgan for helping make this book possible!

JIM BLAKE
Palmers Green
20 April 2015

A BRIEF LOOK AT THE INDIVIDUAL OPERATORS:

THE DISTRIBUTION of Tilling Group fleets around England and Wales was quite uneven, with for instance a concentration of them in East Anglia but few in the South East. They may be summarised area-wise as follows:

1. Greater London:
Eastern National (depot at Wood Green for services to Southend and Canvey Island)
Thomas Tilling Transport (later made a subsidiary of Eastern National)

2. South East:
Brighton, Hove & District
Southern Vectis
Thames Valley, including coaching arm South Midland and subsidiary Newbury & District

3. East Anglia:
Eastern National
Eastern Counties
Lincolnshire
United Counties

4. South West:
Bristol Omnibus Company (including subsidiaries Bath Services and Cheltenham District)
Southern National
Western National
Royal Blue (coaching subsidiary of above two operators)

4. Midlands:
Mansfield District
Midland General, including subsidiary Notts & Derby

5. North West:
Crosville
Cumberland

6. North East:
United Automobile Services, including subsidiary Durham District Services
West Yorkshire

7. Wales:
Crosville
Red & White
United Welsh

The type of bus that typified the Tilling fleets in the 1960s was the Bristol Lodekka, which featured low-height double-deck ECW bodywork with standard transverse seating on both decks. They were mass-produced for all Tilling fleets between 1953 and 1968. Seen at Peterborough Bus Station on Easter Sunday, 22 April 1962, Eastern Counties LFS18 is a 60-seat FS5G, delivered in 1961. It is carrying a good load of passengers on route 151 to Cambridge. Cream window surrounds enhance this Lodekka's smart red and cream livery.

Ideal for the flat countryside of Fenland served by Eastern Counties were their forward-engined Bristol SC4LK single-deckers, with ECW 35-seat bodywork. The first of seventy-seven of these supplied to them between 1956 and 1961, LC502, is seen also at Peterborough Bus Station on Easter Sunday, 1962 working one of the city's local services.

The standard Tilling Group underfloor-engined 30ft long single-decker between 1958 and 1966 was the Bristol MW, again with ECW bodywork. Here on 5/5/62, two of them, MW5G 45-seaters No. 509 & No. 521 dating from 1960, stand at Eastern National's Euston Coach Station, working their limited stop route 322 to Braintree. This operator was unusual in having a number of bus routes which penetrated well into the London Transport Central Area. In addition to the 322, these were the 151 and 251 from Wood Green to Canvey Island and Southend respectively, and the 30 from Bow to Chelmsford. Livery was standard Tilling green and cream. Note the Tilling offices behind the two buses, where bookings could be made for that Kings Cross-based firm's coach tours.

The earlier type of standard Tilling group underfloor-engined single-decker was the Bristol LS. With its ECW body adorned in their green and cream dual-purpose livery, Lincolnshire 1956 LS5G 41-seater No. 2658 has brought a private hire party to London on 1/12/62, and is seen parked in Midland Road, St. Pancras.

The earlier type of Bristol Lodekka was the LD. This is represented by Thames Valley LD5G 60-seater No.781, dating from 1957, seen on 24/4/63 at Victoria Coach Station's fuelling bay. This operator also ran limited stop bus services to London, the A and B from Reading to Victoria. Their livery was red and cream.

More usual on these services by this time were the longer, forward-entrance FLF Lodekkas. This one, brand new FLF6B 70-seater No.868, awaits departure for Reading on service B on 31/5/63. A ride on one of these, particularly on the back seat of the upper deck of these FLF Lodekkas, was an unforgettable experience!

An oddity amongst Tilling Group fleets when seen at Victoria, also on 31/5/63, is South Midland Duple Bella Vega-bodied Bedford SB8 37-seat coach No. C401, which has just been delivered. This operator was Thames Valley's coaching arm and was permitted to purchase these non-Bristol/ECW products since those manufacturers did not produce anything similar.

More typical of coaches supplied to Tilling Group companies at this period was the Bristol MW. MW6G No.720, with the revised style of 39-seat bodywork produced by ECW from 1962 onwards, is on hire to Royal Blue when seen at Victoria the same day. These however were soon superseded by the 36ft-long Bristol REs, with similar-looking bodywork.

In complete contrast, Eastern National open-topper No.1130 is in London after the Epsom Derby that day. It is a Leyland Titan PD1A with very unusual Beadle bodywork, built in 1949 for Westcliffe-on-Sea Motor Services Ltd, whose services and vehicles Eastern National took over in February 1955. The notice in the canopy window tells that it is on hire to Tilling.

A popular type of coach with Tilling fleets just before the appearance of underfloor-engined types was the Bristol front-engined LWL with full-fronted ECW bodywork. Built in 1951, South Midland LWL6B No.609 is the last survivor of this type in its fleet when seen on 26/3/64 in the shadow of the old block of flats which once dominated Victoria Coach Station.

Brand new Eastern Counties Bristol/ECW FS6B 60-seat Lodekka LFS73 stands outside the company's small outstation at Haverhill on 10/5/64. This type of rear-entrance Lodekka was still being produced alongside the longer, forward entrance FLF version at this time.

The standard Bristol/ECW double-deck prior to the appearance of the Lodekka was the Bristol K, and later variants KS and KSW. By 10/5/64 when Eastern Counties 55-seat lowbridge K5G LK374, dating from 1949, was seen at Cambridge Bus Station, these vehicles were rapidly being withdrawn and replaced by new FLF or FS type Lodekkas like the one seen above.

As its model code suggests, the Bristol KSW was an 8ft wide version of the K. These were produced as late as 1957, when Lodekkas had effectively superseded them. On 16/5/64, one of the last produced for Thames Valley, 1954 lowbridge 55-seat KSW5G No.729, arrives at Victoria on a relief journey of service B from Reading.

A day trip to the Isle of Wight on 28/5/64 sees Southern Vectis No. 237 at Carisbrooke Castle. This is a very unusual vehicle for a Tilling fleet, being a 41-seat Duple Vega-bodied Bedford SBO, delivered to them in 1957 for touring work. As with the South Midland Bedford coach seen earlier, delivery of this type was permitted since Bristol did not produce lighter-weight coaches for touring work.

Southern Vectis
No.304 is also seen that day at Carisbrooke Castle. This is a typical Tilling Group Bristol LS6G coach with ECW 39-seat bodywork dating from 1952. Southern Vectis had a monopoly of bus services on the island at this period, other than a route operated between Ryde and Seaview by Seaview Services.

Brighton, Hove
& District was the only Tilling Group operator to serve the south-eastern corner of the English mainland, having originated from the actual Thomas Tilling company. As seen here, their livery was red but with much more cream relief than other Tilling Group operators and almost identical to that of Brighton Corporation with whom services in and around Brighton and Hove were shared. Here on 19/8/64, their 1948 ECW highbridge-bodied Bristol K5G 56-seater No.396 is seen on training duties near their Conway Street depot.

Seen awaiting its crew outside Whitehawk depot the same day, Brighton, Hove & District No.437 is a Bristol KSW6G with ECW 60-seat body dating from 1952. Buses of this type were supplied to BH&D as late as 1957. Note the trolleybus traction standard on the left. Both BH&D and the Corporation had operated trolleybuses in the area.

By 3/10/64, half-cab single-deckers in Tilling Group fleets were becoming quite rare, making this view of three together at Eastern National's Brentwood depot also perhaps quite rare. They are 1951 LWL5Gs No.1128, 1138 and 1137, all with 39-seat ECW rear-entrance bodywork. The LWL was an 8ft wide, 30ft long version of the original Bristol L single-decker, which had first appeared in the late 1930s. It is questionable whether No.1128 had really worked route 251, since this was the main Eastern National route from Wood Green to Southend, at this time worked by 70-seat Bristol FLF double-deckers.

Another Duple-bodied Bedford in South Midland's coach fleet is their No.864, an SB8 with Super Vega 37-seat bodywork built in 1961 seen at Victoria Coach Station on 2/1/65. It is accompanied by a Royal Blue Bristol MW and a Bristol Greyhound Bristol RE coach and had until recently been used on coach tours of Ireland.

Samuelson's depot across the road from Victoria Coach Station was also used for coach arrivals and departures, but here on 13/2/65, Thames Valley 1960 Bristol FLF6G No.837 is unusually parked in its exit. This FLF actually has 65 coach seats, rather than 70 as usual for stage-carriage buses of this type, and was meant specifically for services A and B between London and Reading. The notice on the radiator grille, however, tells how these services are cancelled owing to a labour dispute.

A most unusual coach to be operated by a Tilling Group company is Wilts & Dorset No.904, seen at Victoria Coach Station on 5/6/65. It is a 1952 Leyland Royal Tiger PSU1/15 rebodied by Harrington (with Contender 41-seat bodywork) in 1956 which had been acquired with the business of Silver Star of Porton Down in 1963. The peak above the front indicator blinds had housed Silver Star's emblem.

More mundane at Victoria that day is early ECW-bodied Bristol LS6G 39-seat coach No.1280 in the Royal Blue fleet, new in 1952. It has just arrived after working a relief journey up to London from the West Country. The 'hump' at its rear is a luggage rack, a common feature on this operator's coaches.

Gloucestershire-based Tilling Group operator Red & White was unusual in having a fleet of non-Bristol/ECW coaches built in the early 1950s. One of these, 1952 Duple 37-seat bodied Guy Arab UF UC5-52 has also arrived at Victoria that day, where rebuilding work to enlarge the coach station and provide new office blocks for it is underway.

In common with a number of larger operators, Eastern National bought out the services and vehicles of a number of small independent fleets over the years, thus bringing non-standard vehicles into its standardised Bristol/ECW fleet. One such is 1956 Duple Vega-bodied Commer Avenger III 37-seat coach No.100, acquired with the business of Moore of Kelvedon in 1963. Here it has worked a relief journey on express service X12 to Victoria on 19/6/65. The CN code above its fleetnumber indicates it is based at Eastern National's Clacton depot.

Similar to the Red & White Duple-bodied Guy Arab seen above, their DS9-52 has recently been demoted to dual-purpose status (i.e. suitable for either stage carriage bus duties, or as a coach) and repainted in all-red livery instead of its original cream with red trim. It arrives at Victoria, also on a relief duty, on 26/6/65.

Next day, on Sunday 27/6/65, brand new Eastern National FLF Lodekka 70-seater No.2826 makes a splendid sight awaiting departure from Tilbury Ferry on their long route 53 to Clacton. A London Transport Country Area RT is just visible in the distance.

Surrounded by other Bristol/ECW coaches at Victoria Coach Station on 9/7/65, Eastern National No.309, based at their Prittlewell, Southend depot, is a 1952 LS6G with 39-seat bodywork that had been new to Westcliffe-on-Sea. By now, it is due for withdrawal.

On summer Saturdays, queues of coaches stretched all the way along Buckingham Palace Road and around the corner into Pimlico Road waiting to get into the busy and cramped Victoria Coach Station. One such on 10/7/65 is an unusual visitor – Wilts & Dorset 1954 Bristol LWL5G bus No.553, with a full-fronted ECW 39-seat body, built some three years after underfloor-engined single-deck vehicles had become the norm. This ordinary single-deck bus has been pressed into service on an Associated Motorways express service to London. An early Bristol LS coach with United Automobile Services follows, having come from the North East.

On Sunday 18/7/65, I travelled on an Omnibus Society visit to various operators in East Anglia. Seen in Ipswich Bus Station is a more usual Tilling Group Bristol/ECW front-engined single-decker, Eastern Counties 1948 35-seat rear entrance L5G No. L680.

Also in Ipswich that day is Eastern Counties LL732, a longer Bristol LL5G with 39-seat rear-entrance bodywork new in 1951.

Many buses that had been built during the Second World War with utility bodies were given new bodies in the early post-war years, thus prolonging their lives. One example is Eastern Counties lowbridge Bristol K5G LK244, built in 1945 and given a new ECW 55-seat body in 1953. Interestingly, it has an 8ft wide body fitted to a 7ft 6ins chassis and is seen in Ipswich that day too.

A more conventional Eastern Counties Bristol double-decker from the early post-war years is lowbridge KS5G 55-seater LK284, dating from 1950 and apparently out of service in Ipswich Bus Station.

As mentioned earlier, Eastern Counties had a large batch of Bristol SC4LK single-deckers with ECW 35-seat bodywork. LC546, also at Ipswich Bus Station, dates from 1957.

We also visited Eastern National's Braintree depot and bus station that day. At the latter, 1950 lowbridge Bristol K5G 55-seater No.2270, the last of its batch, awaits departure on local route 312, with a good variety of other Eastern National buses in the background.

Amongst the line-up seen above is 1951 Bristol KSW5G lowbridge 55-seater No.2312, whose smart appearance tells that it has just been overhauled.

Also parked up at Braintree depot that day is 1952 all-Leyland Titan PD2/12 lowbridge 53-seater No. 2117, which had been new to Westcliffe-on-Sea for the famous Wood Green to Southend route 251. It is now spending its twilight years working local services at Braintree.

Even more unusual for a Tilling Group fleet, Eastern National No.2010 is a Guy Arab IV with Northern Counties 63-seat bodywork new to Moore's of Kelvedon in 1957, and acquired by Eastern National in 1963. As the KN garage code shows, it is still based at Kelvedon when seen parked up at Braintree.

On 28/8/65, Southern National 1951 ECW full-fronted Bristol LWL coach No.1334 arrives at Victoria on a Royal Blue service from Swanage.

Royal Blue coaches also worked Associated Motorways services to Birmingham, where their 1952 Bristol LS coach No.1281 accompanies a newer MW type on the following day, Sunday, 29/8/65.

Seen approaching Southend Pier on the seafront on August Bank Holiday Monday, 30/8/65, Eastern National 1949 Leyland Titan PD1A No. 2109 is about to be overtaken by 1947 Titan PD1/1 No.2101. Both have unusual Beadle bodies and were originally new to Westcliffe-on-Sea. I well remember when riding on these beneath the bridge to the pier, the conductor telling people on the upper deck to remain seated owing to the tight clearance. The bridge has been made higher today.

A real oddity with Eastern National, seen in Colchester Bus Station on 7/9/65, is their No.2005, originally a Guy Arab I built in 1943 with a utility body, but rebodied by Massey in 1960 and converted to Arab III specification. It is another of Moore's of Kelvedon's vehicles acquired by Eastern National in 1963.

Two more traditional Eastern National double-deckers at Colchester that day are 1949 lowbridge Bristol K5G No.2243, now due for early withdrawal, and a 1950s LD-type Lodekka. Comparison of the two shows them to be of similar overall height, but the Lodekka has a lower lower-deck floor, permitting the upper deck to be built of normal transverse seating layout, rather than a sunken gangway as on traditional lowbridge buses like the K.

Another Bristol K5G, this time dating from 1950, is Hants & Dorset No.1265, seen at Southampton Bus Station on 19/9/65. Its ECW body, however, is noticeably different from the standard version seen above. This is because it had been built in 1940 and originally fitted to an earlier K, then heavily rebuilt and fitted to a new chassis ten years later. Its front upper-deck windows look decidedly odd, and it seated only 53 as opposed to 55 on the standard K above. Livery of green and cream was exactly the same, though.

Another elderly Hants & Dorset bus at Southampton that day is No.680. This has also been rebodied, being a Bristol LL6B new in 1950, given a new ECW full-fronted, front entrance 37-seat body in 1962 to make it suitable for one-man operation. A variety of other Hants & Dorset vehicles appear in the background. Just visible is its cut-away rear end, to enable it to operate over the Sandbanks Ferry.

Looking much more antiquated, Hants & Dorset No.779, a Bristol LL6G, dates from 1951 but retains its original Portsmouth Aviation rear-entrance 39-seat body and was originally a dual-purpose vehicle. Only two of these remained in service at this time.

Though dating only from 1962, Hants & Dorset Lodekka No.1484 is quite a rarity in that it is a type FL6G – a 30ft, 70-seater with a rear entrance as opposed to the forward one on the more common FLF. Not many of these were built; this operator had six of them. The offside illuminated advertisement panel is also of note. The bus is seen in Southampton city centre.

Back at their Southampton depot, No.1333, a 60-seat highbridge Bristol KSW6G new in 1953, is a more mundane vehicle in the Hants & Dorset fleet!

A visit to Hants & Dorset's Winchester depot on 9/10/65 finds another 1950 Bristol LL6B rebodied in 1962, this time No.682. It too has been adapted for use on the Sandbanks Ferry.

Also at Winchester that day, former Hants & Dorset touring coach No.690 is also an LL6B, dating from 1951, but retains its original coach body and has been demoted to bus status, seating 39. The body is in fact 8ft wide, but mounted on a 7ft 6ins chassis.

Wilts & Dorset was another Tilling Group operator, whose livery was red and cream. Here also on 9/10/65, their No.555 is a Bristol LWL5G, built as late as 1954 with a full-fronted ECW 39-seat front entrance body. It is seen here at their Basingstoke depot.

Also at Basingstoke that day, Wilts & Dorset No.354 is a standard Bristol KSW5G with 55-seat lowbridge ECW bodywork, new in 1952.

With similar red and cream livery, excepting the thin cream band below the upper-deck windows, to the Wilts & Dorset KSW seen above, Thames Valley No.637 is a 53-seat lowbridge KSW6B dating from 1951, fitted with platform doors and meant originally for limited-stop services A and B. It is seen outside Reading General Station on 17/10/65. Note also the difference in front blind layouts between the two buses.

Two earlier Thames Valley Bristol/ECW double-deckers are seen parked at the rear of their Reading depot. No.504 is a K6B dating from 1948 and No.586 a KS6B built in 1950. Both have standard ECW 55-seat lowbridge bodies.

Back at Reading General Station, Thames Valley No. 779 is quite a rarity – a 30ft long rear entrance, 70-seat Bristol LDL6G Lodekka. Not many of these were built, and this was the only one in the Thames Valley fleet. It dates from 1957.

United Counties was another Tilling Group operator, whose buses carried the standard green and cream livery. On 5/3/66, their elderly 1948 lowbridge 55-seat Bristol K5G No.786 calls at Luton Bus Station on local route 56.

Also there that day is their KSW6B No.871, also a 55-seat lowbridge bus, dating from 1951. It works another local service, the 55. Four operators served Luton: United Counties serving most of the countryside north of the town; London Transport Country Area buses and Green Line coaches to the south; Birch Brothers on various services to the north; and Luton Corporation. This latter operator eventually sold out to United Counties.

Seen at Wembley on 12/3/66, Tilling 1958 Bristol MW6B 39-seat coach VYO765 is now the oldest in their fleet and the last survivor in it with this style of bodywork. The fleet has recently been more closely integrated with Eastern National, explaining why it now has the fleet number T300.

An oddity in the South Midland fleet is their No.85, which despite having a 39-seat ECW body of the same style as early Bristol LSs, is actually an AEC Regal IV and was new in 1952. When seen at Victoria Coach Station on 12/3/66, it is due for early withdrawal but has outlasted their Bristol LSs of the same period!

With Victoria Coach Station's ugly new offices as a backdrop, Royal Blue 1953 Bristol LS6G 39-seat coach No.1296 has arrived there on 25/3/66.

Real oddities in a Tilling fleet were the Duple-bodied Guy Arab IIIs with Newbury & District, a subsidiary of Thames Valley taken over in 1950. On 26/3/66, their H13, a 57-seat highbridge example dating from that year, is seen at a rather wet Newbury Bus Station.

With very similar bodywork to the previous vehicle, Newbury & District No.171 is a lowbridge vehicle, seating 53 passengers, also built in 1950. It makes an interesting contrast with the standard Thames Valley Lodekka next to it.

One of the oldest buses still in service with Thames Valley is their No.469, a standard 55-seat lowbridge Bristol K6B dating from 1948, seen in the company of an early 1960s Royal Blue MW coach at Newbury on this gloomy Sunday.

Almost identical in appearance is Wilts & Dorset No.313, a 55-seat K5G dating from 1950 and now one of the oldest in their fleet. It is seen at Andover Bus Station, also on 26/3/66.

Typifying how, during the 1950s and 1960s, old buses were often converted for use as service vehicles, Wilts & Dorset BOW169 seen at their Andover depot is a former L5G bus dating from 1938 now converted to a towing wagon.

Cambridge Bus
Station still looks very wintry on 8/4/66 as Eastern Counties 1953 highbridge 60-seat KSW5G LKH168 lays over there on route 131.

At Newmarket
the same day, Eastern Counties dual-purpose 1955 39-seat LS5G LE762 accompanies 45-seat MW5G bus LM625, which is ten years its junior. The LS looks particularly smart in their cream and maroon coach livery.

At Eastern Counties' Bury St. Edmunds depot the same day, 1951 LWL6B coach LL707, with full-fronted 35-seat bodywork, is one of the last survivors of its type in the fleet. It accompanies another LS dual-purpose vehicle, an elderly L and an LS bus.

1961 FS6G 60-seater LFS21 accompanies an MW single-decker at Bury St. Edmunds Bus Station just around the corner from the depot seen in the previous picture.

At Victoria Coach Station on 14/4/66, Royal Blue 1953 LS6G 39-seat coach No.2200 is one of their last of this type with roof racks, and contrasts with a newer RE coach behind it.

Illustrating how Tilling fleets often downgraded coaches to stage-carriage buses, this Lincolnshire 1952 39-seat LS6G has recently been so converted, painted into their green and cream bus livery and renumbered 2001. It arrives at Wembley for the Schoolboys International football match on 30/4/66.

To illustrate how I would travel through the wind and the rain to visit bus and railway installations throughout the country fifty or so years ago, this picture of Bristol Omnibus Company 1949 L5G 33-seat rear-entrance single-decker No.2492 and 35-seater No.2291 is taken in truly atrocious weather conditions at their garage and central works at Lawrence Hill. They were two of the last of this type still in stock in Bristol's large fleet of standard Bristol/ECW products.

Of similar vintage, K5G highbridge 59-seaters No. 3447 and 3760 are awaiting disposal amongst a group of their fellows at Lawrence Hill Works.

Similar highbridge K5G No.3763, of the subsidiary Bath Services fleet, has also recently been withdrawn.

Nestling between a group of withdrawn K-type double-deckers, 1949 L5G 35-seater No.2284 had latterly been in use as a towing bus, but now it too awaits disposal.

A stranger at Lawrence Hill is Gloucester Services G6006, a 60-seat FSF6B Lodekka of subsidiary fleet Gloucester Services, which is in for repairs. Not many forward-entrance FS type Lodekkas were built; most were the longer FLF version. A typical array of Bristol vehicles forms a backdrop.

Two typical Bristol single-deckers seen at Lawrence Hill are 1953 LS5G 45-seat bus No.2850, and 1965 MW6G 39-seat dual purpose No.2139. The very obviously non-Tilling Group coach on the right is a Southdown vehicle, probably laying over on tour duty.

A very odd vehicle at the works on 8/5/66 is No.2493, a dual-entrance 33-seat L5G single-decker new in 1949. It accompanies one of Bristol Omnibus Company's Bedford vans.

More conventional, in the operational part of Bristol's Lawrence Hill complex, is No.C8061, a 60-seat highbridge KSW. The C prefix indicates that it operates Bristol City joint services in conjunction with the city corporation. By now, it is one of the oldest buses in the fleet.

More typical of the Bristol bus fleet in the mid-1960s is 1959 LD6G 58-seat Lodekka LC8526, also a City services vehicle, seen changing crew outside Eastville garage.

A typical single-decker of the period in Bristol is 1965 MW6G No. 2625, a 45-seater seen outside Muller Road garage.

A visit to Eastern Coachworks' Lowestoft factory on 15/5/66 finds two dual purpose 41-seat MW6Gs awaiting delivery to the Lincolnshire Road Car Company; No.2682 is nearest the camera. On the right stands an unbodied Lodekka FLF chassis, and beyond that two RE coaches.

Lighter Bristol single-deckers were being produced at this time, too, in the shape of the SU. Two of these, Western National No.679 and United Counties No.301, which are both SUL6As, flank Crosville MW6G coach CMS567. The FLF Lodekka on the left is awaiting delivery to Scottish Bus Group fleet Central SMT which, being a nationalised concern, was permitted to purchase Bristol/ECW products. Another unbodied FLF chassis is seen on the right.

Another SUL, this time destined for Southern National, accompanies Midland General FLF Lodekka No.660. This carries blue and cream livery instead of the usual red or green.

In complete contrast to all the new buses and coaches at Eastern Coachworks that day, MXB733 is an AEC Regal I coach supplied in 1952 to Thomas Tilling with full-fronted ECW 35-seat bodywork. Its chassis was one of seven constructed from the parts of eleven pre-war Bristol Tramways Regals! It is in use with ECW's sports club.

On Whit Saturday, 28/5/66, a rather battered-looking Thames Valley 1951 lowbridge KSW6B No.639 arrives at Victoria Coach Station on a relief journey of service B from Reading. The conductor, seen on its rear platform, has probably let his passengers alight while the bus was queuing up in Buckingham Palace Road to enter the coach station! This vehicle was actually designated as a 'coach', intended for services A and B, fitted with 53 coach-style seats instead of the usual 55, and platform doors.

In the coach station itself the same day, beside the recently completed new offices, South Midland No.671, a 1952 39-seat LS6G coach, is now the oldest vehicle in the fleet and has worked up from Oxford.

At High Wycombe's Frogmoor Bus Station on 4/6/66, Thames Valley 1952 LS6G 45-seater No.678 accompanies No.818, a 1950 LL5G rebodied with a full-front 39-seat body in 1958. The bridge in the background carries the former Great Western main line from Paddington to Birmingham and the North West.

Also at High Wycombe, 1952 39-seat LWL6B No.621 stands with 1950 lowbridge K6B No.533, representing the old order in the Thames Valley fleet.

Thames Valley
No.603 is a standard 55-seat lowbridge KSW6B built in 1951, and is seen awaiting departure on route 20 from High Wycombe to Windsor. This ran just outside the operating area of London Transport, who had Country Area bus garages in both towns.

Typical Bristol/ ECW buses in the United Counties fleet, 1952 39-seat rear entrance LWL5G No.412 and 1959 60-seat LD6B Lodekka No.565 stand in Northampton Bus Station on 19/6/66.

In United Counties' Northampton depot, their 1940 K5G JEV420 is now used as a tree-lopper. This had been one of many buses acquired from Eastern National when their North Hertfordshire and Bedfordshire operations were transferred to United Counties in 1950, and had also been rebodied after the war.

In contrast, brand new SUL4A 36-seater No.303, also in the depot, has just been delivered from Eastern Coachworks.

Also at
Northampton, 1950 35-seat rear entrance L5G No.355 has just been withdrawn. It is accompanied by an FS-type Lodekka.

Recently demoted to bus duties at Northampton is 1953 LS5G 39-seat coach No. 439. Of note is the slipboard reading 'Northampton' beneath the windscreen.

One of the oldest double-deckers still in use at this time with United Counties is 1949 K6B lowbridge 55-seater No.800, also seen at Northampton.

Moving on to Kettering, here we see United Counties 1953 45-seat LS6B single-decker No. 469 outside the Town Hall.

Brand new FS6G 60-seat Lodekka No.709 is seen at Bedford Bus Station working route 182 to Hitchin.

A typical group of United Counties Bristol/ECW buses contrast with a City of Oxford AEC Renown at Bedford Bus Station. Nearest the camera are 1952 45-seat LS5G No.450, 1961 FS6B 60-seater No.614 and 1963 FLF6B 70-seater No.634.

At United Counties' Bedford depot is 1946 ex-Eastern National 35-seat rear entrance L5G KNO603, which has been in use since 1961 as a trainer.

Another ex-Eastern National bus at Bedford depot is 1951 KSW5G lowbridge 55-seater No.876, which gleams in the sun when driven out for photographs for members of the Omnibus Society's London and Midlands area branches for whom these visits to United Counties depots were arranged on 19/6/66.

Also posed for us that day is 1965 60-seat FS6B No.678, specially adorned in cream livery to commemorate Bedford Charter Year.

At Midland General's Ilkeston depot on 26/6/66, their No. 316 is a very unusual AEC Regent III with an ECW highbridge 56-seat body of the style usually fitted to Bristol K5s; it is actually in the fleet of their subsidiary Nottinghamshire & Derbyshire Traction Company. Along with Weymann-bodied Regent III 56-seaters No. 318 and No.118, these 1948-vintage double-deckers in Midland General's blue and cream livery are awaiting transfer to Mansfield District, another Tilling Group fleet in the East Midlands. Ironically, No.316 and No.318 were new to that operator in the first place, but transferred to Midland General in 1953.

Also at Ilkeston that day, Midland General No.347 is a 1946 Guy Arab II, originally built with utility bodywork, but rebodied in 1952 with a new ECW 56-seat body. Missing its engine, it now awaits disposal.

Awaiting disposal too are 1938 Weymann-bodied AEC Regal FNN745, latterly used as a towing vehicle, and Mansfield District 1947 Weymann-bodied AEC Regent II 56-seater No.133.

Still in service with Midland General is 1955 43-seat LS6G bus No.234, which was originally a dual-purpose vehicle and is seen at Langley Mill depot.

On 9/7/66, Red & White 1952 Duple-bodied Guy Arab LUF coach UC5-52 squeezes between other coaches as it arrives at Victoria with an Associated Motorways relief journey from Gloucester.

On the same day, this very lucky shot finds Eastern Counties 1951 LWL6B 35-seat coaches LL704 and LL705 together at Victoria. By now, this was the only Tilling Group operator still using this type.

Also quite unusual is Eastern Counties LSC872, one of ten 33-seat SC4LK coaches built for them in 1956/57. It arrives at Victoria with a relief journey from Norwich on 23/7/66.

At a very wet Cheltenham Coach Station on 24/7/66, Red & White 1952 Duple-bodied Guy Arab LUF DS10-52 is in dual-purpose livery, and will be withdrawn at the end of the 1966 season.

In the town of Cheltenham itself, Cheltenham & District L8551 is the first Bristol-built bus in the fleet and was originally numbered L80. It is a 55-seat lowbridge KSW5G new in 1952. Despite being a subsidiary of the Bristol Omnibus Company, this fleet's buses were in a smart maroon and cream livery.

Another Cheltenham & District Bristol is Lodekka No.L8569 (originally L98), a 58-seat LD6B new in 1959. It is seen at their depot. The vents either side of its front blindbox are for its Cave-Brown-Cave heating and ventilation system.

Most well-known in this fleet were their Duple-bodied Guy Arab IIIs, of which by now only two remained in service. One of them is seen here, No. L78 dating from 1950 and seating 57.

On 30/7/66, passengers clamber aboard Red & White Leyland Royal Tiger PSUl/13 dual-purpose vehicle DS53-51 at Victoria. Built in 1951, this had rare, locally-built Lydney bodywork and will soon be withdrawn from service.

It was usual for touring coaches from operators not directly involved in running express coach services to London to be hired to those that did, in order to provide extra capacity during the summer. Here, arriving at Victoria on 5/8/66, Hants & Dorset No.862, a 1957 39-seat LS6G touring coach, is on hire to fellow Tilling Group operator Wilts & Dorset, operating a Royal Blue service from the West Country!

This identical LS6G seen arriving at Victoria the same day is No.1 in the United Welsh fleet, a solitary example delivered in 1956. This fleet at the time had only fifteen touring coaches, the remainder of their vehicles being buses operating in the Swansea area of South Wales. United Welsh began life only in 1938, as a subsidiary of Red & White, to whom this coach is on hire.

Eastern Counties 1951 37-seat LWL6B LL704 is still going strong when seen at the same location that day. The impressive building behind the coach on the other side of Buckingham Palace Road is the British Overseas Airways Corporation's headquarters and coach terminal, for services to and from London's Heathrow Airport.

The large Tilling Group-owned Crosville fleet operated in North Wales and Cheshire, as well as into Liverpool. At their Edge Lane depot in that city on 7/8/66 is their 1953 lowbridge 55-seat KSW6B DKB659, one of their last still in service. This fleet's livery was standard Tilling green and cream.

Several other KSW6Bs are also seen at the depot. Nearest to the camera are DKB480, DKB658 and DKB656, all dating from 1953.

After a weekend in Manchester and Liverpool on the first weekend of August 1966, the following Sunday I was back in the East Midlands on an Omnibus Touring Circle visit to operators in that area. Here on 14/8/66, Midland General 1954 58-seat LD6G Lodekka No.436 stands at Chesterfield Bus Station. The single-decker on the left is an East Midland Leyland Leopard.

A summer holiday spent in Hastings at the end of August 1966 enabled me to visit Brighton again. At Old Steine on 22/8/66, Brighton, Hove & District 1953 60-seat highbridge KSW6G No.460 nicely illustrates that fleet's smart red and cream livery.

Seen in the sun at Harlow Bus Station on 10/9/66, Eastern National 1960 MW5G 45-seat saloon 1343 works their route 49 to its hometown, Bishops Stortford. London Transport Country Area and Green Line services also connected the two towns, but this route strayed beyond their operating area.

An earlier Eastern National single-decker seen the same day is 1955 43-seat L5G No. 1235, which is due for withdrawal. It is seen at their Brentwood garage. This town was odd in that it had an Eastern National garage there serving points to the east and also into Romford, as well as two London Transport Central Area (red) bus routes, the 247 and 287 from Romford, plus the 721 Green Line coach also serving that town and LT Country Area bus route 339 to Ongar, Epping and Harlow!

Also at the garage is 1953 55-seat lowbridge KSW5G No. 2362, which had been new to Westcliffe-on-Sea.

Following the restriction on their being sold only to Tilling Group fleets being lifted, Bristol/ECW vehicles appeared at the Commercial Vehicle Motor Show at Earls Court for the first time in many years in 1966. On 24/9/66, West Yorkshire SRG23 is a RELL6G with dual-entrance 50-seat bus bodywork.

Another visit to High Wycombe's Frogmoor Bus Station, on 28/9/66, finds Thames Valley 1950 LL6B front entrance 39-seater No.568 still in service. It accompanies one of their KSWs. An FLF Lodekka stands behind.

Several LWLs also remained in service at High Wycombe. No.613 is an LWL6B new in 1952 and shows off the alternative 39-seat rear-entrance ECW body style.

Another LWL6B present that day is No.627, also dating from 1952, and stands beside the Great Western main line to Birmingham.

Who in their right mind would go to the Isle of Wight for a day trip on Guy Fawkes Day? Well, I did with a couple of friends to photograph the last steam engines running there! Fortunately, we also visited Southern Vectis! It was a sunny day too, and here at Ryde Esplanade their 1955 60-seat LD6G Lodekka No.511 is working route 1A to Cowes.

A newer Lodekka seen at Ryde, 70-seat FLF6G No.601, dates from 1964 and works route 1, which was quite a busy service following the closure of the railway from Ryde to Newport and Cowes.

At Southern Vectis' Ryde depot, 1952 55-seat lowbridge KSW5G No.764 is stored for the winter. Then, as today, this operator's buses were much busier during the summer holiday season. The notice in the lower deck canopy window warns staff that it is not licensed.

An older K5G stored for the winter at Ryde is No.704, which had been new with a utility body in 1944, and was rebodied with this standard ECW 55-seat body in 1953. By now, it was one of the oldest buses in the Southern Vectis fleet and due for early withdrawal.

Also stored for the winter, 1950 KS5G lowbridge 55-seater No.742 is with a group of other KSs and KSWs outside Ryde depot on 5/11/66.

The evening draws in on 5/11/66 as Southern Vectis 1946 LS5G No.829, which had been given new full-fronted 35-seat ECW bodywork in 1961, accompanies an early 'long apron' LD-type Lodekka at Newport Bus Station.

Also at Newport, 1952 LS6G 39-seater coach No.856 has recently been rebuilt to operate as a stage carriage bus. It had previously been numbered 306. It too accompanies a Lodekka, in this case one of Southern Vectis' 1956 batch of LDs. The coach on the left is one of a number of Duple-bodied Bedfords the company had for touring work.

Swindon was one of the Bristol Omnibus Company's easternmost outposts. At their garage there on 27/11/66 is No.8251, a 'long apron' 58-seat LD6G Lodekka new in 1955.

A later LD6G at Swindon that day is No.8498, dating from 1959 and incorporating the revised radiator grille design for this type.

At Swindon too on that gloomy Sunday is brand new FLF6G 70-seater No.7286, accompanied by a group of other Bristol Lodekkas.

In contrast to the three Lodekkas seen above, Bristol No.307 is a little SUS4A 30-seater used on lightly-trafficked rural services. It is one of a batch of eight built for the operator between 1962 and 1964.

Seen on a misty Saturday, 3/12/66 at Crosville's Crewe depot is 1950 35-seat L5G SLG136, now demoted to training duties. It appears to be missing its rear offside window!

More recent SLB229 is 39-seat LWL6B new in 1951 still in service, and its extra length is apparent when compared to the previous picture.

Also at Crewe that day, 1950 LL5G 39-seaters SLG162 and SLG156 make an interesting contrast with 1956 LS6G dual-purpose 41-seater EUG336, illustrating how ancient half-cab single-deckers look when compared to underfloor-engined, full-fronted types just a few years newer.

Setting off for the village of Sydney on local service K14 as dusk falls on Crewe Bus Station on the same day, 3/12/66, is Crosville 1951 LWL6B SLB271. Single-deckers like this with rear entrances were, of course, still conductor-operated.

By now, Crosville have only a few 1950 K6B 55-seater lowbridge double-deckers in service. DKB392 is also seen departing from Crewe Bus Station.

A more recent Crosville vehicle seen at a snowy Crewe that day is 1954 LD6B Lodekka DLB675. This is one of a batch of eight built to coach specification seating only 52, hence the cream and green livery. It is however working stage carriage route K44 to Nantwich.

On another gloomy winter's day, Sunday, 15/1/67, I travelled down to Bournemouth to visit both the engine shed for Southern steam, and the town's trolleybuses. The main inter-urban and country bus operator there was Hants & Dorset, whose 1952 highbridge KSW6B 60-seater No.1309 stands in the bus station not long after overhaul. Next to it is 1960 FS6G Lodekka No.1447.

An older Hants & Dorset double-decker there is No.1210, a 55-seat lowbridge K6A new in 1949. It was withdrawn a few months after this picture was taken.

Representing older types in their single-deck fleet are 1951 full-fronted LWL6B 39-seater No.696, a coach now relegated to bus work, and No.676, an LL6B originally bodied by Portsmouth Aviation as a coach when new in 1950, but rebodied as a 37-seat bus by ECW in 1961.

Next to them, 1957 LS5G 43-seater single-decker No.807 contrasts with elderly 1949 lowbridge 55-seat K5G No.1251.

Wilts & Dorset buses also served Bournemouth, their red and cream vehicles standing out amongst Hants & Dorset's green and cream ones. This is their 1962 FS6G 60-seat Lodekka No.645 working route 38 through to Salisbury.

I was back in the Midlands on 19/2/67. Here at Midland General's Ilkeston depot is their 1956 LS6G 43-seat single-decker No.244.

Leaving Salisbury Bus Station on 26/2/67 bound for Basingstoke is Wilts & Dorset 1957 LD6G 60-seat Lodekka No.624. Various other standard Bristol/ECW double-deckers are seen on the right at the company's depot.

Salisbury was Wilts & Dorset's main depot, including their overhaul works. Inside it is No.703, a 1958 MW6G 39-seat coach being converted for bus operation.

Also there is their No.537, an LS5G 41-seater dating from 1953. But where is its registration plate?

A much different Wilts & Dorset vehicle is their No.908, a 1960 Harrington Wayfarer-bodied Leyland Leopard L2 41-seat coach acquired from Silver Star of Porton Down in 1963. It arrives at Wembley on 11/3/67 for a schoolgirls' international hockey match.

Also at Wembley for that event on 11/3/67 is Midland General dual-purpose 1959 MW6G 43-seater No.274, looking smart in their cream and dark blue livery.

Back with Hants & Dorset, a visit to their Eastleigh depot on 12/3/67 finds their 1952 LL6B No.784, whose 37-seat body has been rebuilt with a full front to allow one-man operation.

Also at Eastleigh that day, No.674 is a 1950 LL6B which originally had a Portsmouth Aviation rear-entrance body, but was rebodied by ECW in this form, seating 37, in 1961.

Yet another converted Hants & Dorset vehicle at Eastleigh that day is 1952 LS6G 37-seater No.851, downgraded from coach to bus status in 1966.

A more mundane vehicle at Eastleigh depot is 1955 'long apron' LD6G 60-seat Lodekka No.1355.

At nearby Eastleigh Bus Station that day, very smart Hants & Dorset 1966 FLF6B Lodekka 70-seater No.1540 is bound for Southampton.

An older double-decker at the bus station is 1949 55-seat lowbridge K6B No.1231, which will soon be withdrawn. Behind is 1956 LD6G Lodekka No.1372.

Not many Bristol Lodekkas built to 30ft length with rear entrances, of the FL variety, were built – the forward entrance FLF version was far more common. However, Red & White had a batch of twenty FL6Gs delivered in 1960. One of them, L760, emphasises its length at Newport Bus Station on 8/4/67. These had 70-seat bodies, as did the FLFs.

After my day trip to South Wales, next day, Sunday, 9/4/67, I was on another to operators in East Anglia! Here we see at Eastern Counties' Peterborough garage their highbridge K5G LKH245. This is something of an oddity, being originally delivered in 1945 with utility bodywork. It was rebodied in 1953, and the 55-seat body is 8ft wide but mounted on a 7ft 6in chassis. A look at its nearside wheels clearly illustrates this. By now, it was due for early withdrawal.

In Peterborough
City Centre, one of
Eastern Counties'
many 35-seat
SC4LKs, LC555 which
was one of twelve
delivered to them in
1959, is seen on local
service 305.

At Peterborough's
somewhat windswept
Bus Station beside
the River Nene, one
Eastern Counties'
large single-deckers,
standard MW5G
LM976 dating from
1959, has a good
load of passengers
aboard on route 343
bound for March.
The building in
the background is
Peterborough Lido.

Representing Eastern Counties' modern double-deckers at the same location is 1965 60-seat FS5G LFS115.

Our next port of call that day was Eastern Counties' March garage. Inside is 1954 LS5G 39-seater LS759, by now downgraded to work stage-carriage bus services, but still bearing coach livery.

An oddity at March garage that day is LL744, the prototype Bristol/ECW LS single-decker, built in 1951 and seating 41. Unusually, it has only a four-cylinder engine and is termed LSX4G. Strangely, Eastern Counties had few standard Bristol LS buses, just a batch of five dual-purpose LS4Gs (again unusual) built in 1952, three dual-purpose LS5Gs dating from 1955 and four 45-seat LS5G buses delivered in 1957 plus thirteen LS5Gs dating from 1953-55 transferred from Eastern National in 1966. Instead, in the mid/late 1950s, their standard single-decker was the SC4LK prior to the arrival of MW5Gs from 1958 onwards. Fortunately, the prototype LS seen here survives in preservation, but its 'growling' appearance was not perpetuated on the production models!

Out of use at March that day are 1948 standard 56-seat highbridge K5Gs LKH220 and LKH403. These had been renumbered from LKH82 and 90 to make way for new FSs in 1964.

Also apparently out of use with them is lowbridge 55-seat KS5G LK300, dating from 1950. Once again, despite having a 7ft 6ins wide chassis, its body is 8ft wide, though in this case, the bus was provided with this body when new.

A day trip on 23/4/67 to Southampton finds Hants & Dorset No.678 near the docks. This is a 37-seat LL6B new in 1950 and rebodied by ECW in 1962. The cut-away rear end is for working across the Sandbanks Ferry.

At Southampton Bus Station the same day, standard lowbridge K6B No.1235 dates from 1949, but carries its original 55-seat body. It arrives on route 41 from Eastleigh.

1952 37-seat LL5G No.785 has been rebuilt with a full front to allow one-man operation, rather than being rebodied. It too is seen at Southampton Bus Station.

Posed for the photographer at Hants & Dorset's Southampton depot is open-topper No.1109. This is a Bristol K6A dating from 1945, but carrying a Brush 59-seat body built in 1937.

Another Bristol K6B dating from 1950 and seen at Southampton depot is Hants & Dorset No.1265. Its ECW body, however, is noticeably different from the standard version seen above. It had been built in 1940 and originally fitted to an earlier K, then heavily rebuilt and fitted to this new chassis ten years later. Its front upper-deck windows look decidedly odd, and it seated only 53 as opposed to 55 on the standard K above.

Hants & Dorset No.783, a rebuilt LL6B 39-seater dating from 1951, shows its revised front entrance arrangement, and accompanies 1956 LD6G 60-seat Lodekka No.1379.

Another K5G with a heavily-rebuilt body is FRU827, originally fleet No. TD782 and now relegated to driver training duties.

Representing the standard ECW early post-war 55-seat lowbridge bodywork fitted to most Ks, KS6B No.1275 dates from 1951.

Southampton depot also housed Hants & Dorset's main works, where 1957 LS6G 39-seat coach No.860 is undergoing conversion to work as a bus. Beside it is an MW built in 1966.

At Wembley on 29/4/67, similar Eastern National 1957 LS6G 39-seat coach No.323 arrives with spectators for a sporting event.

By 6/5/67, Victoria Coach Station was becoming busy again with the onset of the summer season. South Midland No.677, a 1952 39-seat LS6G coach, is now one of the oldest vehicles in the fleet and has worked up from Oxford.

Brighton's Old Steine on 7/5/67 is the setting for this view of Brighton, Hove & District No.474, a 60-seat highbridge KSW6G new in January 1955. One of their newer FLFs passes on the right.

Recalling a batch of Duple-bodied Bedford SBOs delivered to them in 1954, brand new Eastern Counties Bedford VAM CB837 has Duple 'Viceroy' bodywork, and is seen also in Brighton on 7/5/67.

Also at Brighton that day, 1956 Harrington Wayfarer-bodied Leyland Tiger Cub PSUC1/2 41-seat coach is another that had passed from Silver Star to Wilts & Dorset as their No.906, but is now in the livery of their recently-acquired subsidiary Shamrock & Rambler of Bournemouth.

Another Brighton, Hove & District KSW6G highbridge 60-seater seen that day is No.489, new in 1956. It is seen near their Hove depot.

In the depot itself, similar KSW6Gs No.444 and 445 are part of a line up. They date from early 1953.

Basingstoke town centre is being redeveloped on 13/5/67 as Wilts & Dorset 1953 55-seat lowbridge KSW6B No.388 sets off on local route 105.

Thames Valley worked into Basingstoke too. Here, their 1958 LS5G 41-seat single-decker S327 works route 6B to Reading. This had recently been acquired from United Welsh, as whose No.107 it was one of five of a batch supplied that year.

After a trip to record steam on the London & South Western Main Line early that day, I was back at Wembley in time to catch Thomas Tilling's 1961 Duple Vega-bodied Bedford SB8 7BXB arriving there for yet another sporting event!

A trip to Bristol Omnibus Company's Lawrence Hill depot and works on 14/5/67 sees their FLF Lodekka No.6008 which has now, however been transferred to fellow Tilling Group fleet Southern National.

Bristol Greyhound was the fleet name for BOC's coaching fleet, used on Associated Motorways express services and touring work. Also at Lawrence Hill is 1955 LS6B 39-seat coach No.2882, last of a batch of twenty-five built between 1953 and 1955.

Representing Bristol's standard LS buses, No.2885 is a 45-seater dating from 1956 also seen at Lawrence Hill.

At this period, plenty of Bristol KSWs were still operating for Bristol Omnibus Company and subsidiaries. Nearest the camera is Bristol City Services' C8085, last of a batch of fifty delivered in 1951/52, standing alongside 8081 of the same batch but new for Bristol's inter-urban services.

Seen while undergoing body and mechanical repairs is No.2884, new in 1955 and first of a batch of thirty-four 45-seat buses delivered in 1955-57.

Older Bristol double-deckers used for driver training at Lawrence Hill are lowbridge K5G 55-seater No.L4122 new in 1949 and highbridge 60-seat KS6B C3477, a City Services bus new in 1951.

1951 KS6B C3468 is also a driver trainer, and this view shows the difference between this highbridge double-decker and a more modern FLF-type Lodekka.

A later highbridge Bristol City Services double-decker is C8227, a KSW6B dating from 1955. It too contrasts with a Lodekka.

Also dating from 1955, KSW No.8345 is a Bristol Omnibus Company bus used on inter-urban services, as its blind showing Weston-super-Mare as its destination implies.

This splendid FLF 70-seat forward-entrance Lodekka, No. LC8540, was the first in their fleet, a prototype new in 1960. The grilles either side of the blind-boxes are for its Cave-Brown-Cave heating system. It was our means of transport to visit various Bristol Omnibus garages in the City on our tour.

A later Bristol Omnibus Company FLF, No.6012, is seen at their Muller Road depot.

Passing the depot is smartly turned-out City Services KSW 60-seater C8163 on route 83, from the Old Market to Cheltenham Road.

Similar KSWs C8076 and C8066, dating from 1951, appear to be out of use at this depot. It was usual for buses to run in service with their original operators for 15 or 16 years at this period.

The tour also took us to Bath, where BOC subsidiary Bath Services' L8086 is seen at their depot. This is one of ten lowbridge 55-seat KSWs supplied in 1952, and now due for early withdrawal. It accompanies 1959 LD Lodekka C8455.

Possibly the oddest vehicle with any Tilling Group operator at this period is ex-Silver Star Trojan minibus 367BAA, which Bath Services used on special tours connecting Bath's famous Roman Pump House and Assembly Rooms. It is seen in Bath depot.

Back outside in the yard is 1951 highbridge KSW No.8030, soon due for withdrawal, and BOC's first production LD Lodekka, complete with long apron, No.L8133 dating from 1953.

A contrast between Bath Services lowbridge and highbridge KSWs is provided by 55-seater L8095 dating from 1952, and highbridge 60-seater No.8266 of 1955 vintage.

Back at Victoria Coach Station on 27/5/67, it is the busy Whitsun Bank Holiday weekend as Western National 1952 LS6B coach No.1350 arrives working a Royal Blue service from the West Country.

In London for a sightseeing trip after the 7/6/67 Epsom Derby is Hants & Dorset open-topper No.1111, another 1945 Bristol K6A with 1937 59-seat Brush bodywork.

At Basingstoke Bus Station on 10/6/67, Wilts & Dorset 1952 lowbridge 55-seat KSW5G No.358 is parked with two of the fleet's Lodekkas, an FLF and an LD type.

Also there that day is their 1953 LS5G 41-seat single-decker No.534.

I was surprised early in the morning of Sunday, 11/6/67 to find Eastern National 1965 FLF6B 70-seat Lodekka No.2845 parked just around the corner from home in select Georgian Canonbury Square! It is presumably working a private hire.

A visit to Midland General on 11/6/67 finds their 1948 Weymann-bodied AEC Regent III 56-seater No.324 at Langley Mill garage. It had been new to Mansfield District.

A more standard vehicle for a Tilling Group fleet is their 60-seat highbridge KSW6G No.305, new in 1953. It bears the livery of subsidiary fleet Notts & Derby, which however is the same as Midland General's blue and cream.

With similar ECW bodywork to the KSW above, No.104 is a Guy Arab II new in 1945 originally with utility bodywork, but given this new 56-seat body in 1952.

No.106 is another Guy Arab II rebodied by ECW in 1952. Midland General had six of these buses, whose chassis/body combination was very rare indeed!

Midland General
No.91 is one of six highbridge Weymann 56-seat AEC Regent IIIs delivered new to the company in 1948.

Representing Weymann's
lowbridge 53-seat bodies on AEC Regent III chassis, No.424 is one of a batch of ten delivered to Midland General in 1950. A further twenty virtually identical buses originally intended for this fleet were diverted to London Transport, becoming their RLH1-20.

Another splendid old AEC with Midland General is AEC Regal III No.176, with Weymann 35-seat bodywork. This was new to Mansfield District in 1949 and transferred to Midland General in 1958. Of note are the initials 'MGO' (Midland General Omnibus) on its radiator in the position usually occupied by the AEC blue triangle. The Regents in this fleet also had this feature.

Mansfield District No.89 is a 1948 Weymann 56-seat highbridge AEC Regent III which has recently been transferred from Midland General. It is seen outside Mansfield's Sutton Road depot. Livery is green and cream, and this Regent has the initials 'MDT' (Mansfield District Traction) in its radiator triangle.

A later Regent III with Mansfield District is No.165. New in 1954, it has Crossley 60-seat highbridge bodywork, and is one of four acquired from local operator Bevan & Barker in 1957.

For a change, here is a standard Tilling Group vehicle in Mansfield District's fleet! No.202 is a 39-seat ECW-bodied Bristol LS6G new in 1954, one of just six coaches in the fleet and used for touring and private hire work.

At this time, the first rear-engined Bristol VRs had appeared, and HHW933D is a demonstrator on hire to Mansfield District when seen calling at the stop opposite their depot in Sutton Road. Its ECW bodywork is very similar to the FLF Lodekkas then still being built, but once one-man-operated double-deckers were permitted to operate, this type quickly replaced earlier Bristols in former Tilling Group fleets during the 1970s.

Back to Mansfield District's earlier vehicles, No.159 is a 1948 AEC Regent III with Brush 56-seat bodywork, one of three acquired from Ebor Bus Services in 1950.

Out of commission in Mansfield District's depot is 1949 Weymann-bodied 35-seat AEC Regal III No.15, of the same batch as the one with Midland General seen earlier.

An older AEC Regal seen at Mansfield is GRR261, now fitted for snowplough duties, though judging by the flat tyre on its nearside front wheel it seems not to have been used for some time!

We saw 1948 Weymann-bodied AEC Regent III 56-seater No.318 earlier, awaiting transfer from Midland General to Mansfield District, with whom it is now operating. This is quite odd, since the bus was new to them in the first place, until transfer in 1953. The two fleets were closely linked anyway, and by now had a common vehicle numbering system.

An unusual shot taken on 18/6/67 is this one of Crosville 1950 LL6B 39-seat single-decker SLB177 working a Crewe local service near Newcastle-under-Lyne. It is taken through the rear window of a coach I was travelling on visiting Potteries Motor Traction depots in the area. This was the easternmost fringe of Crosville's bus operations.

Another enthusiasts' tour on 25/6/67 took me to various United Counties depots. The first was Aylesbury, where their No.932, a 1954 55-seat KSW6B is laying over.

With the same bodywork, but dating from 1952, KSW6B No.897 has been working service 61 to Tring, which took a less direct route to there from Aylesbury than the two London Transport services linking the towns, Country bus 301 and Green Line 706.

At United Counties' Luton depot, No.909 is another 55-seat KSW6B, dating from 1953. It contrasts with a 1964-built FS-type Lodekka No.667.

United Counties' earliest Bristol Lodekka is LD6B No.950, the first of ten 'long apron' 58-seat versions delivered in 1953/54. It is also seen at Luton.

At Luton too is No.879, a KSW5G 55-seater which had been new to Eastern National in 1952 but transferred to United Counties in May of that year when the former operator's services, vehicles and depots in and around Aylesbury, Bedford and Luton were transferred to them, almost doubling the size of the fleet!

An earlier Bristol at Luton that day is No.800, a lowbridge 55-seat K6B new in 1949.

Former Eastern National 1946 L5G No. 317 has now been demoted to driver training duties.

An earlier Bristol L-type single-decker has now been more drastically converted into this breakdown tender and towing wagon, number 18 in the service vehicle fleet.

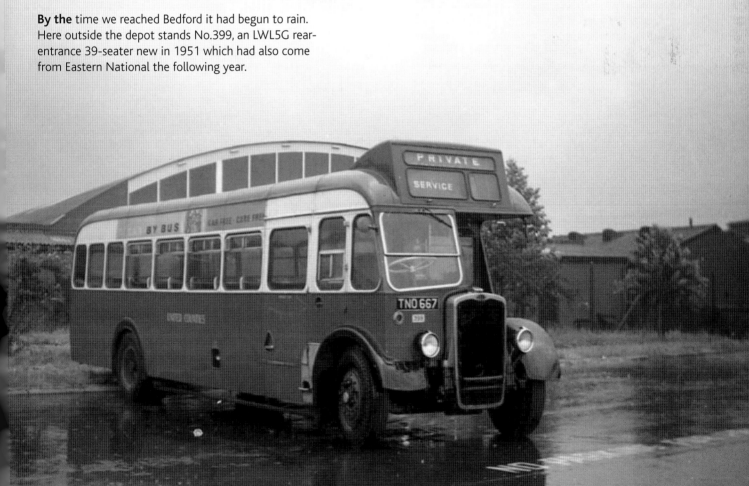

By the time we reached Bedford it had begun to rain. Here outside the depot stands No.399, an LWL5G rear-entrance 39-seater new in 1951 which had also come from Eastern National the following year.

Another LWL5G 39-seater, No. 409 new to United Counties in 1952, appears to have come to grief and had to be towed home to Bedford!

At United Counties' Biggleswade depot, United Counties 1948 lowbridge K5G No.786 calls for a crew change on route 224 bound for Huntingdon. The Duple 'Firefly'-bodied Bedford coach beside it is our tour vehicle.

Posed for us outside the depot is No.442, an LS5G 45-seat saloon supplied to United Counties in 1952.

At the same spot, No.835 is a 55-seat lowbridge KS5G new in 1951.

Looking smart, No.472 is one of five dual-purpose LS6B 45-seaters new to United Counties in 1953.

Brand new FLF Lodekka No.731 makes a splendid sight outside Biggleswade depot, contrasting with an ex-Eastern National KSW inside the shed.

Also seen inside the shed are 1950 KS5G No.837, and 1951 No.840, carrying an 8ft wide body on a 7ft 6ins chassis. Though their 55-seat ECW lowbridge bodies are of the same design, the fact that No.840's is six inches wider than 837's is quite apparent.

Ex-Eastern National 1950 KS5G No.826 is not, of course, really working the famous Eastern National route 251 from Wood Green to Southend, but buses of this batch could perhaps have done so, two of them still being with that operator when the bus was posed outside United Counties' Biggleswade depot for us! It seems odd that it had the destination 'Southend' on its blinds, or did one of our party bring the blind specially?

Back up north in Birkenhead on 1/7/67, Crosville DKB641 is a 55-seat lowbridge KSW6B new in 1953, part of the last batch (of thirty) buses of this type bought by that operator. It is working local route F19 from Birkenhead to Heswall, via Pensby.

Also in Birkenhead working the local F13 to Liverpool is Crosville SLG221, an LWL5G 39-seater new in 1951.

At Crosville's
Birkenhead Rock
Ferry depot is
DKB431, a 60-seat
highbridge KSW6B
new in 1951.

Also at the Rock
Ferry depot is
Crosville's SLB186, a
39-seat LL6B new in
1950.

One of the wider LWL6Gs new in 1951, SLG224 passes Birkenhead Bus Station on local service F4, which ran to Frodsham via Ellesmere Port and Hellsby. It also seats 39. The buses in the background are those operated by Birkenhead Corporation.

Lowbridge Crosville KSW6B DKB633, one of thirty new in 1953, sets off from Birkenhead Station for Heswall on route F19.

Also at the station is EUG310, an LS6G new in 1952 as a coach, and subsequently converted to dual-purpose for routes such as the F89, from here to Cranage Hospital.

A trip to Lincoln on 15/8/67 finds Lincolnshire Road Car Company No.2477 in the city centre. This is an SC4LK 35-seat new in 1960 and one of almost 100 of these buses in the fleet. As with those with Eastern Counties, these light single-deckers were ideal for working in the flat countryside of the Fenlands.

On the same day, United Counties 1956 LS5G 45-seater No.105 is seen in Stamford. This once important market town on the old Great North Road was served by three Tilling Group operators: Eastern Counties, Lincolnshire and United Counties.

The city of Carlisle was served by four major operators' bus services in the 1960s: BET fleet Ribble; Tilling Group fleets Cumberland; and United and Western SMT of the Scottish Bus Group. On 27/8/67, smart Cumberland 1965 FLF 70-seat Lodekka No. 531 has a good load of passengers aboard as it awaits departure from Carlisle Bus Station.

An older Bristol double-decker seen in Carlisle the same day is United Automobile Services' 1953 60-seat highbridge KSW6B BBH34. Despite being based primarily in the North East, this operator did have a depot in Carlisle, as we shall see later.

Also in the United fleet in Carlisle is 1958 MW5G 45-seater BU514.

With two other MWs in the background, United BU232 stands in their Carlisle depot. It is an LS5G, also with 45 seats, dating from 1957.

Back at Carlisle Bus Station, Cumberland No.558 is an FS Lodekka dating from 1962.

Another United LS5G, BU189 dating from 1956, arrives in Carlisle on 29/8/67.

In the historic city of Chester on a very wet 1/9/67 is Crosville CSG663, an SC4LK with 33-seat coach bodywork new in 1960.

1951 LWL5G
SLG215 arrives in Chester city centre the same day, with a newer MW single-decker in pursuit.

LWL5G SLG213
of the same batch passes beneath Chester's Northgate. The vehicle following is a Chester Corporation Massey-bodied Guy Arab IV.

Another Guy with Massey bodywork is Eastern National No.2016, one of two built in 1961 for Moore's of Kelvedon and acquired by them in 1963. It is an Arab IV with a 67-seat lowbridge body and is seen at a very wet Colchester Bus Station on Sunday, 3/9/67.

Amid a group of typical Eastern National ECW-bodied Bristols on the same occasion are 1953 55-seat KSW5G No.2368, 1955 'long apron' LD5G 60-seat Lodekka No.2443, and 1958 LD5G No.2512, also a 60-seater. A few years later, the KSW would be one of those featured in the On the Buses comedy films, painted red rather than its original green!

The coach used for our Eastern National Enthusiasts' Group tour that day was the company's unique Yeates 'Europa'-bodied Commer Avenger IV 41-seat coach No.102, which had been new to Moore's of Kelvedon in 1960. Here it stops specially for photographs on the way from Colchester to Clacton.

Outside Eastern National's Clacton garage that day is 1958 MW5G 45-seat saloon No.1301.

Early 'long-apron'
LD5G Lodekka
2422 is seen here at
Dovercourt. It is part
of a batch of twenty-
three new to Eastern
National in 1954 and
seats 58.

Also at a rather wet
Dovercourt is MW5G
45-seater No.1306,
new in 1958. Quite
what the purpose of
the 'Transit Camp' for
which it is blinded
is unclear; probably
this was one of
the many military
establishments in the
area.

Of the same batch, 1958 MW5G No.1304 is accompanied by other typical Bristol/ ECW vehicles in Clacton Bus Station.

Back in the North West, Crosville DKB657, a 55-seat lowbridge KSW6B new in 1953, stands at Liverpool's Pier Head on 9/9/67.

The next day, 10/9/67, finds West Yorkshire 1956 dual purpose 41-seat LS5G SUG33 from the other side of the Pennines on an outing to Blackpool.

I hope readers will forgive me for including this rather gloomy shot of Eastern National 1956 LD5G 60-seat Lodekka No.2480. It has just departed from their route 30's Bow terminus for Chelmsford, and passes Bow Road Station on the evening of 29/9/67. This was the last journey of this traditional route, which was withdrawn west of Romford next day.

On 1/10/67, United Counties 1965 FS6B Lodekka 60-seater No.678 stands at Oxford Bus Station while working route 31 to Bedford, which was jointly operated with BET fleet City of Oxford Motor Services.

Also at Oxford Bus Station that day is Thames Valley No.852, a dual-purpose MW6G 41-seater new in 1960. Working route 5 to Reading, it is one of only four single-deckers in their fleet to carry this dual-purpose red and cream livery.

West Yorkshire
1953 55-seat KSW6G DGW8 is seen beneath the trolleybus wires at Bradford's Forster Square on 7/10/67. A Corporation tower wagon noses in on the left.

Seen in Bradford Bus Station the same day, West Yorkshire SBW33 is an LWL6B 39-seater dating from 1952, seen in the company of an LS saloon.

Also at the bus station, the same company's SMG11 is a 1954 LS5G 45-seat saloon, sporting a somewhat uninformative blind display!

A visit to Thames Valley's Reading depot on 8/10/67 finds United Welsh 1959 LD6G Lodekka No. 297 which has just been acquired by this operator.

At Wembley
on 2/3/68, West
Yorkshire 1955
LS6G 39-seat
coach CUG18
arrives for that
year's Schoolboys
International football
match.

Similar-looking
United Counties
coach No.203 is a
later MW6G model,
also seating 39, a
solitary example built
for them in 1961.

At Wembley the following week is Tilling's T302, a 34-seat MW6G built in 1961, with the later style of ECW coach body, making an interesting contrast with the Duple-bodied Bedford coaches either side of it.

At Midland General's Ilkeston depot on 28/4/68 is their 1953 KSW6G highbridge 60-seater No.408, carrying Notts & Derby livery.

On the same occasion, we see their 1955 LS6G 43-seat saloon No.237.

Seen in Epsom on Derby Day, 29/5/68, Eastern Counties 61-seat open-topper LKD239 is a 1953 KSW5G recently transferred to them from Eastern National.

Seen outside Brighton Station on 8/6/68 is Brighton, Hove & District KSW6G highbridge 60-seater No.497, new in December 1953.

On 29/9/68, this South Midland LS6G 37-seat coach heads along the Uxbridge Road through Ealing working their Oxford to London express service via High Wycombe. This had recently been transferred from Eastern National, to whom it was new in 1957.

At Wilts & Dorset's Andover depot on 14/7/68, No.561 is an LWL5G with full-fronted ECW 39-seat bodywork new in 1954.

In complete contrast, No.903 is one of three ex-Silver Star Leyland Tiger Cub PSUC1/2s with unusual Harrington dual-purpose 41-seat bodywork built in 1957/58 and acquired from Silver Star in 1963.

Also at the depot, No.335 is a 55-seat lowbridge KSW5G new in 1952 and now relegated to training duties.

A visitor from neighbouring fleet Hants & Dorset is 1959 MW6G 39-seater No.870, recently downgraded from coach to bus status.